CW00801550

Basics in Lace

This book is dedicated to Betty, Helen and Val (who were my inspiration), and to all the other knitters who are willing to give the challenges in life a go.

Vicki Moodie.

Copyright: R & V Moodie   1996

ISBN 0 9587593 5 9

Published by

CRAFT MOODS
P.O. Box 1096
CABOOLTURE Qld. 4510
Australia
Phone/Fax (07) 5496 6826
www.craftmoods.com.au

Printed by   NICHOLSON PRINTERS Pty Ltd
6C 43 Industrial Avenue
Morayfield Road
CABOOLTURE Qld. 4510

Phone (07) 5495 1371
Fax (07) 5498 3783

10/99

CONTENTS

ABBREVIATIONS

K	knit	sts	stitches
P	purl	stst	stocking stitch
st	stitch	tog	together

Stocking stitch (stst): Knit one row, purl one row.

GENERAL INSTRUCTIONS

YARN REQUIREMENTS
8ply acrylic yarn has been used for all projects except No13 (Potpourri dolly) which uses a small amount of 4ply cotton. Most small projects can be made from scrap yarn, while most of the larger projects require less than 100g of yarn.

HOW TO KNIT IN LACE
From the left, place lace to back of work, insert needle into the first stitch and through first eyelet hole in lace, yarn over needle and complete the stitch. Keep the tension loose. Follow this procedure to the end of the row and cut off lace only.

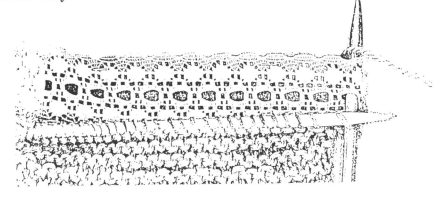

HOW TO NEATEN ROWS and JOIN LACE
To neaten ends of lace rows, overlap lace towards you by one hole at the beginning and the end of the row. To join eyelet lace part way through a row, just overlap each piece of lace by two sets of holes.

HOW TO FORM SINGLE SIDED EYELET LACE
If single sided eyelet lace is unavailable in the colour you desire, choose quality double sided eyelet lace and cut lengthwise below the holes to form single sided lace.

TYPES OF EYELET LACE (actual size)

Double sided (90 holes per metre)

Fine single sided (100 holes per metre)

Fancy 7cm wide (120 holes/m)

FANCY WIDE EYELET LACE
Because fancy wide eyelet laces vary in the number of holes per metre, depending on the header lace, the number of holes required has been given with each pattern using this lace. Metreage required is determined by the number of holes given, divided by the number of holes per metre. Check this with your stockist.

METHODS TO COVER COAT-HANGER HOOKS

1. Thread 4mm plastic tubing over hook and finish with a plastic tip.

2. Thread hook with 1.5cm wide gathered lace (with a header large enough to insert the wire hook) and glue into place.

3. Knitted in lace:
   > Cast on 25sts.
   > Knit 3 rows.
   > Knit in a row of double sided eyelet lace. Cast off.
   > Right sides out, sew cast-on and cast-off edges together. Thread over hook and sew or glue into place.

4. Wrap hook with 6mm wide ribbon and glue ends into place.

1. FLY SPRAY MAN (fits 250g pressure pack fly spray)

---

8 ply yarn (dark, light and flesh for pants, shirt and face)
pr 4mm knitting needles
1.8m double sided eyelet lace (pants)
1.2m double sided eyelet lace (shirt)
20cm of 6mm wide ribbon
12mm chenille stem
pr 12mm oval eyes
black felt
shirring elastic
craft glue

PANTS

Turn all lace under by 2 holes at ends.

Using dark yarn, cast on 14sts.

Knit 2 rows.

Row 3. K1, knit dark coloured lace into 12sts, K1.

Knit 5 rows.

Repeat last 6 rows nine more times. (10 rows of lace)

Knit 3 rows. Cast off.

SHIRT

Using light coloured yarn, right side of work facing, pick up every second st at the side of the pants. (32sts)

Knit 6 rows.

Row 7. Knit in a row of light coloured lace.

Knit 3 rows.

Repeat last 4 rows twice more. (3 rows of lace)

Knit 2 rows.

FACE

Change to flesh coloured yarn and beginning with a knit row, work 12 rows of stst. Cast off.

Right sides together, join centre back seam using the appropriate colours of yarn. Turn right side out. Sew a row of stitching in light coloured yarn down the centre front of the pants. Using Figure 1 (Page 23), cut 2 base/feet from black felt. Glue them together then sew them into the base of the pants.

Thread double thickness shirring elastic through the cast-off sts of the head. Place knitting over can, pull up the elastic and tie off. Cut the 12mm stem to fit around the can and glue this over the cast-off edge for hair. Glue on eyes and other features made from felt. Make a bow from the 6mm ribbon and glue at chin.

2. BUNNY IN A HOOP

8 ply yarn
pr 4mm knitting needles
3.8m double sided eyelet lace
60cm of 6mm wide ribbon
12cm jointed bunny
15cm embroidery hoop
flowers

DRESS

Cast on 36 sts.

Row 1. Knit in a row of lace.

Knit 3 rows.

Row 5. Knit in a row of lace.

Row 6. (K2 tog, K4) to end. (30sts)

Knit 2 rows.

Row 9. Knit in a row of lace. (3 rows of lace)

Row 10. (K2 tog, K3) to end. (24sts)

Knit 2 rows. Cast off.

SHOULDER STRAPS (Make 2)

Cast on 12sts.

Knit in a row of lace. Cast off.

HOOP COVER

Cast on 87sts.

Knit 3 rows

Row 4. Knit in a row of lace.

Repeat last 4 rows once more. (2 rows of lace)

Knit 2 rows. Cast off.

Right sides together, sew back seam of dress. Turn right side out and place on bunny. Sew shoulder straps at waist. Decorate dress with a bow.
Place hoop cover over embroidery hoop and sew cast-on and cast-off edges together. Twist this seam to the back. Using 30cm of ribbon, make and attach a hanger. Sew and glue bunny into position. Decorate the hoop with flowers.

3. BEAR TOILET ROLL HOLDER

8ply yarn
pr 4mm knitting needles
8.8m double sided eyelet lace
30cm of 6mm wide ribbon
14cm jointed bear
flowers
toilet roll

DRESS

Cast on 60sts.

Row 1. Knit.

Row 2. Knit in a row of lace.

Knit 3 rows.

Repeat last 4 rows eight more times. (9 rows of lace)

Row 38. Knit in a row of lace. (10 rows of lace)

Row 39. (K2 tog, K4) 10 times. (50sts)

Knit 2 rows.

Row 42. Knit in a row of lace.

Row 43. (K2 tog, K3) 10 times. (40sts)

Knit 2 rows.

Row 46. Knit in a row of lace. (12 rows of lace)

Row 47. (K2 tog, K2) 10 times. (30sts)

Knit 2 rows.

Row 50. Knit in a row of lace. (13 rows of lace)

Row 51. (K2 tog, K4) 5 times. (25sts)

Knit 2 rows. Cast off.

SHOULDER STRAPS

Cast on 12sts. Knit in a row of lace. Cast off.

Right sides together, sew centre back seam of dress. Turn right side out. Place over toilet roll. Insert bear into roll. Keeping centre back seam to back, pin and sew shoulder straps into place. Decorate with ribbons and flowers.

4. COAT-HANGER (Red)

8ply yarn
pr 4mm knitting needles
1.3m (152 holes) of 7cm wide fancy eyelet lace (120 holes/m)
1m of 6mm wide ribbon
adult size wooden coat-hanger
4mm plastic tubing for hook
wadding
flowers (optional)

Note: Overlap lace by 2 holes at ends.

Cast on 71sts.

Knit 7 rows.

Row 8. Knit in a row of wide lace (holes to the *top*, wrong side of lace facing).

Knit 2 rows.

Row 11. K1, (yarn forward, K2 tog) repeat to end. (35 ribbon holes)

Knit 5 rows.

Row 17. K1, (yarn forward, K2 tog) repeat to end. (35 ribbon holes)

Knit 2 rows.

Row 20. Knit in a row of wide lace (holes to the *bottom*, wrong side of lace facing).

Knit 7 rows. Cast off.

Cover the hanger with wadding. Right sides together, sew side seams. Turn right side out. Place cover over hanger and sew cast-on and cast-off edges together. Insert and secure ribbons from the outside towards the centre, through both sets of ribbon holes together. Join ribbon at centre and finish in a bow. Sew wide lace together at side edges. Cover hook with plastic and decorate cover.

5. COAT-HANGER (Green)

8py yarn
pr 4mm knitting needles
1.3m (152 holes) of 7cm wide fancy eyelet lace (120 holes/m)
1.2m double sided eyelet lace
1m of 6mm wide ribbon
adult size wooden coat-hanger
wadding
flowers

Work as for coat-hanger (red) Pattern 4, rows 1 - 11.

Knit 2 rows.

Knit in a row of double sided lace.

Knit 2 rows.

Row 17. K1, (yarn forward, K2 tog) repeat to end. (35 ribbon holes)

Knit 2 rows.

Row 20. Knit in a row of wide lace (holes to the **bottom**, wrong side of lace facing)

Knit 7 rows. Cast off.

HOOK COVER

Make as for method 3 on page 5, but do not make up yet.

Cover the hanger with wadding. Right sides together, sew the side seams. Turn right side out. Insert and secure ribbons. Place cover over hanger and sew cast-on and cast-off edges together. Sew wide lace together at side edges. Slip hook cover over wire hook and sew in place. A touch of glue may be necessary at the end of the hook to hold the knitting in place.

6.   CHECKERBOARD CUSHION

100g each light and dark coloured 8ply acrylic yarn
pr 4mm knitting needles
14m double sided eyelet lace
500g fibre fill
40cm calico
3 press studs

STRIPES 2 and 4. (make 2)

Using light coloured yarn, cast on 13sts.

Knit 26 rows.

Change to dark coloured yarn and knit 3 rows.

Row 30. Knit in a row of lace.

Knit 3 rows.

Repeat last 4 rows four more times.

Row 50. Knit in a row of lace. (6 rows of lace)

Knit 2 rows.

Change to light coloured yarn, and repeat the last 52 rows once more, *changing to dark coloured yarn as before for the lace square.*

Using light coloured yarn, knit 26 rows. Cast off.

STRIPES 1, 3 and 5. (make 3)

Using dark coloured yarn, cast on 13sts.

Knit 3 rows.

Row 4. Knit in a row of lace.

Knit 3 rows.

Repeat last 4 rows four more times.

Row 24. Knit in a row of lace. (6 rows of lace)

Knit 2 rows.

Change to light coloured yarn and knit 26 rows.

Change to dark coloured yarn and repeat the last 52 rows, *changing to light coloured yarn for the knitted square.* (12 rows of lace)

Change to dark coloured yarn and knit 3 rows.

Knit in a row of lace.

Repeat last 4 rows four more times.

Knit in a row of lace.

Knit 2 rows. Cast off. (16 rows of lace)

Sew stripes together as per Figure 2 (Page 23). Place back and front right sides together. Sew together three sides and all of the 4th side except a 20cm central opening. Turn right side out. Sew press studs at opening. Make a fabric insert cushion using two 40cm squares of fabric. Sew together as before, leaving an opening for the fibre fill. Stuff with fibre fill, then sew opening closed. Place fabric insert into cushion cover and fasten the studs.

7. BRIDAL BETTY

8ply yarn
pr 4mm knitting needles
17.2 m double sided eyelet lace
60cm of 10mm wide ribbon
25cm of 6mm wide ribbon
10cm pearls on a string
tulle 30cm x 30cm (veil)
30cm high doll
2 press studs
sewing thread
flowers

DRESS

The dress is worked sideways in one piece, beginning and ending at the centre back seam.

Cast on 36sts.

Knit 2 rows.

Row 3. K27, turn. (The holes at each turn form the ribbon holes.)

Row 4. Knit a row of lace into these 27sts.

Row 5. K27, turn.

Row 6. K27.

Row 7. Knit.

Row 8. K9, knit lace into the remaining 27sts. (2 rows of lace)

Repeat last 8 rows twice more. (6 rows of lace)

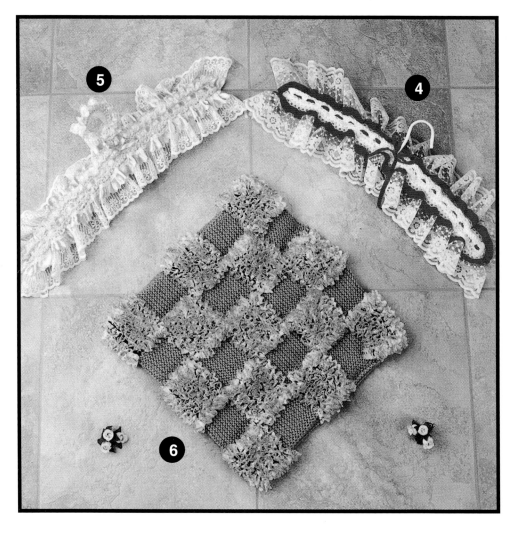

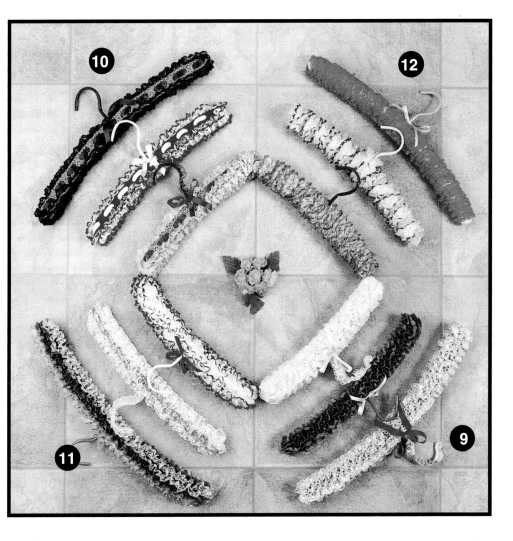

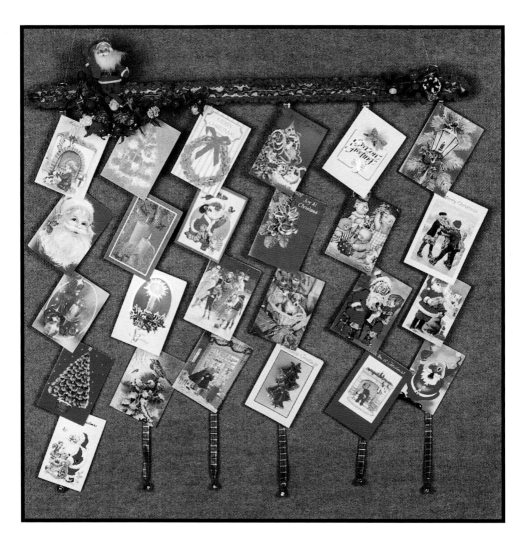

Row 25. K29, put the remaining 7sts onto a stitch holder, turn. (armhole)

Row 26. Knit.

Row 27. Knit, turn work, then cast on 7sts. (36sts)

Row 28. K9, knit lace into the remaining 27sts. (7 rows of lace)

Repeat rows 1 - 8 six more times. (19 rows of lace)

Repeat rows 25 to 28 once more. (20 rows of lace)

Repeat rows 1 - 8 three more times. (26 rows of lace) Cast off.

ARMHOLES

With right side of work facing, beginning at the underarm, pick up and knit 3sts across the armhole, 7sts at front of armhole and 7sts at back of armhole. (17sts in all) This will join the top shoulder. Knit in a row of lace. Cast off. Work second armhole the same.

DRESS TRAIN

Cast on 13sts.

Knit 2 rows.

Row 3. Knit in a row of lace.

Row 4. K1, increase in next st, knit to last 2sts, increase in next st, K1. (15sts)

Knit 4 rows.

Repeat the last 6 rows ten more times. (11 rows lace and 35sts)

Row 69. Knit in a row of lace. (12 rows of lace)

Row 70. K1, K2 tog, knit to last 3sts, K2 tog, K1. (33sts)

Repeat row 70 four more times. (25sts)

Row 75. Knit in a row of lace. (13 rows of lace) Cast off.

Right sides together, sew underarm and shoulder seams of dress. Turn right side out. Sew press studs to centre back opening of dress. Sew cast-on sts of dress train to the back of the dress, below the ribbon holes. Thread the 10mm ribbon through the ribbon holes with the ties to the back. Using the 6mm ribbon, tie a bow around Betty's neck. Dress Betty, tie dress bow, add a necklace of pearls and a bouquet of flowers.
To make the veil, fold the tulle over by one third and hand gather 1cm from the fold. Pull up and secure the gathers to suit. Glue or pin veil to the hair. Decorate if desired.

8.   DOLLY DUSTER

8ply yarn
pr 4mm knitting needles
8.5m double sided eyelet lace
50cm of 6mm wide ribbon
small doll 20cm high
feather duster approx 30cm long
5 minute araldite
rubber band

This project is knitted in garter stitch.

Cast on 66 sts.

Knit 2 rows.

Row 3. Knit in a row of lace.

Knit 3 rows.

Row 7. Knit in a row of lace.

Repeat last 4 rows twice more. (4 rows of lace)

Knit 2 rows.

Row 18. (K9, K2 tog) 6 times. (60sts)

Row 19. Knit in a row of lace.

Knit 2 rows.

Row 22. (K8, K2 tog) 6 times. (54sts)

Row 23. Knit in a row of lace. (6 rows of lace)

Knit 2 rows.

Row 26. (K7, K2 tog) 6 times. (48sts)

Row 27. Knit in a row of lace. (7 rows of lace)

Knit 2 rows.

Row 30. (K6, K2 tog) 6 times. (42sts)

Row 31. Knit in a row of lace.

Knit 2 rows.

Row 34. (K5, K2 tog) 6 times. (36sts)

Row 35. Knit in a row of lace. (9 rows of lace)

Knit 2 rows.

Row 38. (K4, K2 tog) 6 times. (30sts)

Row 39. Knit in a row of lace. (10 rows of lace)

Knit 3 rows.

Knit in a row of lace.

Repeat last 4 rows once more. (12 rows of lace)

Row 48. Knit.

Row 49. K7, K2 tog, K12, K2 tog, K7. (28sts)

Row 50. K7, increase over next st, K12, increase over next st, K7. (30sts and armholes made)

Row 51. Knit in a row of lace. (13 rows of lace)

Knit 3 rows.

Row 55. Knit in a row of lace (14 rows of lace completed). Cast off loosely.

HAT

Cast on 30sts.

Row 1. Knit in a row of lace.

Row 2. Knit.

Row 3. Knit in a row of lace. (2 rows of lace)

Row 4. (K2 tog) to end. (15sts)

Row 5. Knit.

Row 6. K1, (K2 tog) 7 times. (8sts)

Row 7. Knit.

Run the thread through the remaining sts and pull up. Sew the back seam of the hat. Sew the hat to the head. Cut the legs off the dolly at the knees. Glue the dolls buttocks to the handle of the duster with araldite. Hold in place with a rubber band until dry.
Right sides tog, sew the back seam of the dress. Turn right side out, and place over doll and duster. Gather up neck edge to fit, then secure. Tie ribbons at waist (below the second last row of lace) with a bow at the front.

Projects 9 - 12

BACK TO BASICS COAT-HANGERS
(Baby, Child and Adult)

Although the knitting in lace craze started many years ago with the knitting of coat-hangers, we have been asked for basic hanger patterns. Following are four basic patterns for baby (child, adult) coat-hangers.

Make up: Cover the hanger with wadding. Right sides together, sew the side seams. Turn right side out then insert the hanger. Sew cast-on and cast-off edges together. Decorate as desired.

Requirements: Each hanger will need the requirements listed below, plus any specific items listed with each pattern.

8ply acrylic yarn
pr 4mm knitting needles
suitable ribbons and flowers for decorating
4mm plastic tubing and tip for hook cover
wooden coat-hanger
wadding

---

9. BASIC HANGER

2.7m (3.1, 3.9m) 90 holes/m double sided eyelet lace

Cast on 44sts (52, 67sts) and knit 3 rows.

Row 4. Knit in a row of lace.

Repeat the last 4 rows four more times. Cast off. (5 rows of lace)

Make up.

10. BASIC HANGER (with ribbon holes)

1.6m (2, 2.4m) 90 holes/m double sided eyelet lace
1m of 10mm wide ribbon

Cast on 43sts (55, 67sts) and knit 3 rows.

Row 4. Knit in a row of lace.

Knit 3 rows.

Row 8. * K1, yarn forward, K2 tog, * repeat from * to * to last st, K1.
(14, 18, 22 holes)

Rows 9 - 11. Knit.

Repeat rows 4 - 11 once more. (2 rows of lace and 2 rows of ribbon holes)

Row 20. Knit in a row of lace. (3 rows of lace) Cast off.

Thread the holes with ribbon allowing for the stretch in the knitting, then make up.

11. STRIPED HANGER

1.6m (1.9, 2.4m) each of 2 colours of 90 holes/m double sided eyelet lace

Cast on 44sts (52, 67sts) and knit 3 rows.

Row 4. Knit in a row of *first colour* of lace.

Knit 3 rows.

Row 8. Knit in a row of *second colour* of lace.

Repeat last 8 rows twice more. (6 rows of lace) Cast off. Make up.

12. SIDEWAYS HANGER Great for scraps of lace.

3.4m (4, 5.4m) 90 holes/m double sided eyelet lace

Cast on 12sts and knit 3 rows.

Row 4. Knit in a row of lace.

For baby hanger: repeat rows 1 - 4 nineteen more times. (20 rows of lace)

For child hanger: repeat rows 1 - 4, twenty three more times. (24 rows of lace)

For adult hanger: repeat rows 1 - 4, twenty six more times. (32 rows of lace)

Knit 3 rows. Cast off.

Make up in a similar manner to the other basic hangers.

13. POTPOURRI DOLLY

4ply cotton
pr 3.25mm knitting needles
1.1m single sided eyelet lace (110 holes/m)
25cm of 1.5mm wide ribbon
potpourri and fibre fill
small 8cm tall doll
very small flowers

NOTE: When knitting in the lace, the holes of the lace are to the top.

Cast on 5sts.

Row 1. Purl.

Row 2. Knit, increasing in every st. (10sts)

Row 3. Purl.

Row 4. Knit, increasing in every st. (20sts)

Row 5. Purl.

Row 6. Knit (increasing in next st, K1) 10 times. (30sts)

Row 7. Knit in a row of lace.

Rows 8, 9 and 10. Knit.

Row 11. Knit in a row of lace. (2 rows of lace)

Knit 2 rows.

Row 14. (K3, K2 tog) 6 times. (24sts)

Row 15. Knit in a row of lace. (3 rows of lace)

Knit 2 rows.

Row 18. (K2, K2 tog) 6 times. (18sts)

Row 19. Knit in a row of lace. (4 rows of lace)

Beginning with a knit row, work 4 rows of stocking stitch.

Row 24. K4, yarn forward, K2 tog, K7, yarn forward, K2 tog, K3. (armholes)

Row 25. Purl. Cast off.

Right sides together, gather up cast-on stitches. Sew the back seam, then fill skirt with potpourri and fibre fill. Insert the doll, then gather up the neck edge of dress and secure.

Thread 1.5mm wide ribbon through the waist stitches, then pull up and tie in a bow at the front. Make a hanger from 4ply cotton and attach to back of dress. Glue the flowers to the head for a hat.

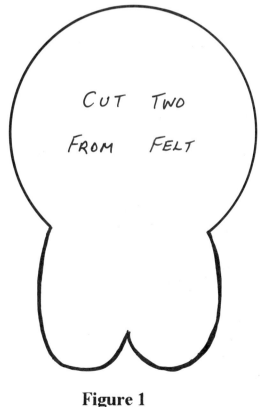

CUT TWO

FROM FELT

Figure 1

Stripe No

1	2	3	4	5
Lace		Lace		Lace
	Lace		Lace	
Lace		Lace		Lace
	Lace		Lace	
Lace		Lace		Lace

Figure 2

14. CHRISTMAS CARD HOLDER

8ply white acrylic yarn
pr 4mm knitting needles
4.9m each red and green double sided eyelet lace 90holes/m
6m of 15mm wide tartan ribbon
miniature pegs or paper clips
90cm dowel (broomstick)
Christmas decorations
2 x 25mm rings
6 x 10mm bells
wadding

Cast on 140sts.

Knit 3 rows.

Row 4. Knit in a row of *red lace.* (overlap lace by 2 holes at ends)

Knit 3 rows.

Row 8. Knit in a row of *green lace.* (overlap lace by 2 holes at ends)

Repeat last 8 rows two more times. Cast off. (3 rows of red lace, 3 rows of green lace)

Wrap a strip of wadding around the dowel. Cut 6 ribbon lengths each 1 metre, then sew and glue them to the wadded dowel, 4cm from each end and about 15cm apart.
Right sides together, sew side seams (narrow ends) of knitting. Turn right side out. Place knitting over wadded dowel, pulling the ribbons free, sew together the cast-on and cast-off edges. Sew the two rings to the back of the dowel (ensuring that the stitches are sewn to the wadding and the knitting), 10cms from each end of the dowel. Attach a bell to the bottom of each ribbon. Decorate with Christmas decorations. Using paper clips or miniature pegs, hang the cards from the ribbons.

15. HELEN HARPIC BEAR

2 colours of 8ply yarn
pr 4mm knitting needles
9m double sided eyelet lace 90 holes/m
55cm contrast double sided eyelet lace (apron)
50cm of 6mm wide ribbon
1.3m of 5mm wide ribbon
500g harpic bottle
20cm bear parts
5 minute araldite
flower

BODY (use main colour eyelet lace)

Using main colour yarn, cast on 10sts.

Row 1. (increase in next st, K1) 5 times. (15sts)

Rows 2, 4, 6, 8 and 10. Knit.

Row 3. K1, (increase in next st, K1) 7 times. (22sts)

Row 5. (increase in next st, K1) 11 times. (33sts)

Row 7. (increase in next st, K2) 11 times. (44sts)

Row 9. (increase in next st, K3) 11 times. (55sts)

Row 11. Knit in a row of lace.

Knit 3 rows.

Repeat last 4 rows five more times. (6 rows of lace)

Row 35. Knit in a row of lace.

Knit 2 rows.

Row 38. (K3, K2 tog) 11 times. (44sts)

Row 39. Knit in a row of lace. (8 rows of lace)

Row 40. (K2, K2 tog) 11 times. (33sts)

Knit 2 rows.

Row 43. Knit in a row of lace. (9 rows of lace)

Knit 3 rows.

Row 47. Knit in a row of lace. (10 rows of lace)

Repeat last 4 rows three more times. (13 rows of lace)

Next row. K1, (yarn forward, K2 tog) 16 times. (16 ribbon holes)

Knit 1 row. Cast off loosely.

SLEEVES (make 2)

Using main colour yarn, cast on 14sts.

Row 1. Knit in a row of main coloured lace.

Knit 3 rows.

Repeat the these 4 rows, three more times. (5 rows of lace) Cast off.

Right sides together, sew base and centre back seam of body. Turn right sides out. Place over the harpic bottle. Thread 50cm of 6mm wide ribbon through the ribbon holes and pull the ribbon up to the groove of the bottle, then tie in a bow at the centre.

Right sides together, sew underarm seam of sleeves. Turn right sides out, insert arm pieces, and sew sleeves to body (between the second and third top rows of lace). Remove sufficient stuffing from head piece to allow the lid of the bottle to be inserted. Glue head in place with araldite.

APRON (use contrast eyelet lace)

Using contrast yarn, cast on 20sts and knit 24 rows.

Row 25. K1, K2 tog, K14, K2 tog, K1. (18sts)

Rows 26, 28 and 30. Knit.

Row 27. K1, K2 tog, K12, K2 tog, K1. (16sts)

Row 29. K1, K2 tog, K10, K2 tog, K1. (14sts)

Row 31. K1, K2 tog, K8, K2 tog, K1. (12sts)

Leave these 12sts on the needle. Using the spare needle, pick up and knit in a row of lace in the 16sts down the side edge of apron, across the 12sts on hold, and up the 16sts of other side edge. (44sts) Cast off.

Thread 60cm of 5mm wide ribbon through the cast-on stitches and tie at the waist of the bear body. Thread ribbon through the lace holes at the apron edge. Sew in place. Make 2 small bows and sew in place on apron. Glue a flower in the bear's ear. The clothes are fully removable for laundering.

16. SOAP ON TAP COVER

8ply yarn
pr 4mm knitting needles
4.4m of double sided eyelet lace 90 holes/m
50cm of 6mm wide ribbon
250ml Colgate Palmolive soft wash container

Cast on 10sts.

Row 1. (Increase in next st, K1) 5 times. (15sts)

Rows 2, 4, 6, 8 and 10. Knit.

Row 3. K1, (increase in next st, K1) 7 times. (22sts)

Row 5. (Increase in next st, K1) 11 times. (33sts)

Row 7. (Increase in next st, K2) 11 times. (44sts)

Row 9. (Increase in next st, K3) 11 times. (55sts)

Row 11. Knit in a row of lace.

Knit 3 rows.

Repeat last 4 rows four more times. (5 rows of lace)

Row 31. Knit in a row of lace.

Knit 2 rows.

Row 34. (K3, K2 tog) 11 times. (44sts)

Row 35. Knit in a row of lace. (7 rows of lace)

Row 36. (K2, K2 tog) 11 times. (33sts)

Row 37. K1, (K2 tog, yarn forward, K2) 8 times. (8 ribbon holes)

Knit 4 rows. Cast off loosely.

Right sides together, gather up cast-on stitches at base, sew side seam, then turn right side out. Thread the ribbon through the ribbon holes. Place the knitting over the soap container, pull up ribbon and secure with a bow.